TALKIN' MOTOR SPORTS

BY JAMES BUCKLEY JR. • ILLUSTRATED BY JAMES HORVATH

The Child's World®
childsworld.com

Published by The Child's World®
1980 Lookout Drive • Mankato, MN 56003-1705
800-599-READ • www.childsworld.com

Photos: Cover: ssuaphotos/Shutterstock.
Interior: AP Image: John Raoux 21. Newscom: Jeff
Siner/TNS 5; Adam Levine/Icon SW 11; Carl Juste/
TNS 14; David J. Griffin/Icon SW 17B. Joe Robbins:
9, 19. Shutterstock: Action Sports Photography 1, 4,
10, 12, 18; TOSP 6T; Suradech Prapairat 6B;
Christian Delbert 7; Photo Works 8; Chen WS 12;
Philip Rubino 15; Ahmad Faizal Yaha 15; Bojack 17.

ISBN 9781503835771
LCCN 2019943135

Printed in the United States of America

TABLE OF CONTENTS

INTRODUCTION

In motor sports, there's an old joke. When was the first car race? The answer is "when the second car was built." People have been racing cars ever since cars were invented in the late 1800s. Today, fans watch powerful machines race all over the place.

Call me "Gearhead." That's slang for a racing fan!

Name the Game: Motor, Car, or Auto?

Racing sports use all of those names. Motor sports include anything raced on land with a motor. Car and auto mean the same thing: a four-wheeled driving machine.

Caption here

Alphabet Soup

NASCAR

National Association for Stock Car Auto Racing

IndyCar

Indianapolis-style Car Racing, American open-wheel racing

F1

Formula 1, an open-wheel group based in Europe

MX

Motocross, a popular form of motorcycle racing

I won 200 NASCAR races. That's the most of all time!

◄ Petty raced from 1958 to 1992. Today, he owns a NASCAR racing team.

Famous Drivers

You watch your favorite stars on the track today. Here are some heroes from the past.

A.J. Foyt (IndyCar)

Mario Andretti (IndyCar and F1)

Juan Fangio (F1)

Richard Petty (NASCAR)

GEAR UP

Motor sports can be exciting and fun to watch. The cars speed around the track. The engines roar! But the sports can be dangerous. Drivers wear lots of gear to keep them safe.

▲ *Head to toe, drivers wear gear that helps protect them in case of an accident.*

Helmets

All motor sports drivers and riders wear hard helmets. The insides have thick pads to protect drivers. Thick plastic shields cover the driver's face. Wires connect the helmets to radios. Some types even have straws for sipping water! Racing is hot and sweaty work!

Fire suits

Race car drivers wear one-piece jumpsuits. The suits are usually covered with colorful labels. Those are the companies that give money to help the racer's team. The suits are made of material that will not burn. This protects the drivers from fire.

Why "stock cars?" That means race cars that look like a car you might own!

The Vehicles

If it can roll, people race it! NASCAR races stock cars. Those are made to look a bit like an everyday car. Stock cars are much faster than what your family drives! Open-wheel racers look like rockets with tires. They are long and thin. The wheels do not have covers. Wings at the back of these cars make them safer to drive. Dragsters race in short, straight races. Some dragsters have wheels as tall as the car! Motorcycles of all kinds are also raced. Some speed by on hard tracks. Others churn the dirt in stadiums.

ON THE TRACK

These are the "over the wall" pit crew members!

Most car races are held on hard tracks. The surface is sort of like a street, except smoother. The tracks can be circles or ovals or full of many twists.

Wave the Flags

Every racer wants to see the checkered flag. The black-and-white flag is waved when a race winner crosses the finish line first. A green flag means go. It starts the race. A yellow flag means "slow down." It comes out when there is an accident on the track.

In the Pits

Cars need gas to race. They sometimes need new tires, too. Other times, they break and need fixing. Race teams do all that work in the pits. Experts leap into action when their driver stops. Pit crews can fill a tank with gas and change four tires in less than 15 seconds!

▼ Walls and Fences

To protect the fans, tracks have strong walls and high fences. The walls form the outside of the tracks. They also help the drivers know where and when to turn.

▲ Not Just Asphalt

Not every race is on a hard surface. Motorcycles can race on dirt and even ice! Snowmobiles zoom along on snow, of course.

▲ Parking Lot

The center of the track is called the infield. Here, teams park the trucks that carry the cars from race to race.

IN THE RACE

Racing seems pretty easy. Everyone starts at the same time. Whoever finishes first is the winner, right? That's true, but a lot happens in between start and finish.

▲ *Here's the start of a NASCAR race. The cars line up in two long rows. The car on the right front in this picture is in the "pole position."*

Qualifying

How do races choose who starts first? Most types of racing hold **qualifying** races. These are held a day or two before the actual race. Drivers see who can put up the fastest speeds alone on the track. The top speedsters start at the front of the race. The fastest car earns the "pole" position.

On the Grid

After qualifying, the racing lineup is set. It's called a starting **grid**. In a NASCAR race, 43 cars are on the grid. They line up in rows of two. About 25 cars start an IndyCar or F1 race, also in rows of two.

Hey, look! That's actor Matt Damon! At some races, celebrities wave the green flag that starts the race.

Go! Go! Go!

Most car races begin with the cars rolling. The starting grid drives slowly around the track a few times. Then the green flag waves. The cars **accelerate!** That means they hit the gas and reach top speed! The start is one of the most exciting moments in any race!

The racers spin around and around the track. Some cars are faster than the others. Who will end up in first place? Let the race begin!

The red-and-white striped section shows the drivers where not to drive!

▲ *The start of a Formula 1 race can be crowded. Soon the field of drivers will spread out.*

In the Pack

Stock car races feature tight packs. Cars race at top speed just inches from each other. Cars sometimes even get bumped! Drivers have to be ready to react in an instant. Open-wheel racing is a bit more wide open. Cars still get close, but usually only in the tight turns.

Drafting

On the highway, it's wrong to tailgate. That means to drive too close to the car in front of you. On the racetrack, it's just fine! In racing, this is called drafting. Racers drive very close to another car. The car in front cuts through the air. The car behind drives through smoother air.

Passing

Drafting helps a stock car driver get ready to pass. He can swoop out and zoom past the car in front. That's called a slingshot pass. In open-wheel racing, passing is much harder. Drivers need nerves and skill to make a pass. Their tires are just inches apart!

Victory Lane!

Every driver wants to end the race here. The race winner's car is pushed to this special spot near the track. The driver gets a trophy. He celebrates with his crew and his family. It's the happiest place in racing!

SPEED RULES!

The most important stat in racing is wins. Whoever has the most is usually the fastest. Racers also measure other things, though.

Points!

Every race has a winner. Every racing season has a champion. During the year, racers earn points for where they finish. Winners earn the most points each race. At the end of the year, racers with the most NASCAR points join a playoff. The final four meet in the last race of the year. Whoever is farthest ahead is the season champ. In IndyCar and Formula 1, the season points leader is the champion.

Laps

A lap is one complete trip around a track. Each race has a set number of laps. Racers can also earn points by being ahead during a lap. Fans look for who led the most laps in a race, too.

A NASCAR race uses up more than 5,000 gallons (18,927 l) of fuel!

Speed

Car speed is measured in miles per hour (mph). Racers reach much higher speeds than you do in your car, though! NASCAR racers can sometimes go more than 200 miles (322 km) per hour. Formula 1 races are sometimes slower, because they have more turns. In the straightaways, though, they can hit 180 mph (290 kph).

RACING PEOPLE

One person is in the driver's seat or on the motorcycle saddle. They're not alone on race day, though. Many people work hard to help a machine win. Others make sure the fans have fun and stay safe.

Pit crew

This group of experts makes sure race cars keep rolling. The cars enter the pits several times in each race. Crew members go "over the wall." They change tires and put in more fuel. They have to work fast. Every second counts in racing! Pit crews train for hours for just seconds of work.

▲ *In the garage, expert mechanics work on a racing motorcycle. Besides the driver, racing teams might have dozens of people working at every event.*

Safety and Fire

Accidents can happen during races. Just in case, safety workers are ready to go. Firefighters have hoses and trucks ready. Tow trucks go on the track to haul away wrecks. Doctors and paramedics are ready to help injured drivers.

Engine Experts

Cars are complicated machines. They have thousands of parts. Mechanics make sure all the parts are working just right. They work on the car for many hours before a race. Some parts can be checked with computers. Others need a big wrench and strong hands to check. Drivers know mechanics are important teammates.

Flag Waver
This worker has fast hands! He stands in a booth above the finish line. He waves green, yellow, or checkered flags. He spins them so that he looks like a colorful top!

FUN STUFF

▼ *This picture is not tilted.*
It's the track that is "banked."

Racing has lots of fun words and phrases. Use these the next time you're watching a race with friends. Listen to the TV announcers, too. They might teach you some new ones!

apron

No, it's not something a chef wears! On a racetrack, the apron is the hard surface right next to the actual track.

banking

Some racetracks have sections that are angled or tilted. These are called banks.

bite

This means how well tires grip a racetrack.

crew chief

The head of the pit crew and the mechanics.

In Great Britain, a car's trunk is called "the boot."

deck lid
In NASCAR, that's the name of the place where the trunk would go (if there was one!).

drop the hammer
When a racer stomps on the gas pedal to go faster.

Grand Prix
This means *grand prize* in French. It is the name given to most races in Formula 1.

hairpin
A very sharp turn in a racetrack.

lug nuts
You won't find these in snack mix! These are metal parts that hold a tire to the car.

paddock
In open-wheel racing, this is where the cars are worked on before a race.

slicks
Race tires that do not have a tread.

▼ Racing tires are called slicks. The slick on top has had a "blowout."

MORE SLANG

Watching the Christmas tree, a hotshoe aims for a photo finish!

See how many of these words or terms you hear or read when you follow your favorite racers.

blip
A little tap on the gas pedal.

Christmas tree
The set of colored lights that helps start a drag race.

donuts
When a driver spins a car in circles in celebration.

hole shot
In motorcycle racing, this describes when a racer sprints between others to reach the front at the start.

hot shoe
Slang for a very fast driver.

jack man
The pit crew member who uses a tool called a jack to raise the car.

loose
Drivers use this term when their car is not steering correctly.

off-road
A type of racing that takes place in the wilderness, not on paved tracks.

marbles

Rubber that has fallen off tires and collects alongside the track

pace car

The vehicle that drives in front of a grid of cars; it leaves the track as soon as the green flag is waved.

photo finish

A race that ends with cars so close together that only a photo can show who won!

restart

The term for beginning a race again following an accident.

switchback

An S-shaped curve in a racetrack.

transporter

A huge truck that carries race cars from track to track.

▲ *Only this photo showed that the white car won. It happened too fast for anyone to see!*

GLOSSARY

accelerate (ak-SELL-er-ate) to add power so that a car goes faster

accident (AK-sih-dent) in racing, a crash by one or more cars

complicated (KOM-plih-kay-ted) difficult, or made of many parts

grid (GRID) a set of lines that form a checkerboard pattern

jumpsuits (JUMP-soots) one-piece clothing that completely covers the arms, legs, and body

mechanics (muh-KAN-iks) experts who repair engines

pits (PITZ) area of a racetrack where cars are serviced during a race

qualifying (KWAL-ih-fy-ing) the process of earning a starting spot in a race

tailgate (TAYL-gate) to drive too close behind a moving car

FIND OUT MORE

IN THE LIBRARY

Kortemeier, Todd. *Superstars of NASCAR.* Mankato, MN: Amicus Ink, 2017.

Silverman, Buffy. *How Do Formula One Race Cars Work?* Minneapolis, MN: Lerner Books, 2016.

You Got This! (Nitro Circus series). New York, NY: Ripley's Believe It Or Not, 2019.

ON THE WEB

Visit our Web site for links about motor sports:

childsworld.com/links

Note to Parents, Teachers, and Librarians: We routinely verify our Web links to make sure they are safe and active sites. So encourage your readers to check them out!

INDEX

About the Author and Illustrator

James Buckley Jr. is the author of more than 100 books on sports for young readers, as well as many sports biographies. He lives in Santa Barbara, California. James Horvath is an illustrator and cartoonist based in California. He has written and illustrated several children's books, including Dig, Dogs, Dig! and Build, Dogs, Build!